PASTA BOOK

BY GENNARO CONTALDO

PENGUIN BOOKS

PHOTOGRAPHY BY DAVID LOFTUS

HI GUYS, JAMIE HERE!

Welcome to Gennaro Contaldo's fantastic seasonal pasta book. I'm sure most of you know Gennaro already – he's one of the most illustrious, talented and flamboyant Italian cooks on the planet. He was my first boss when I moved to London and the first person to show me how to cook Italian food in a truly authentic way – to be honest, he's totally shaped the last 20 years of my career. He's my best friend, my mentor, and we've enjoyed cooking together all over the world ever since.

This little book is the fourth in a collection of no-nonsense, beautiful cookbooks, inspired by the incredible cooks, chefs and artisans on my Food Tube channel. If you don't know the channel already, hunt us out on YouTube, where myself and a bunch of super-talented people – including Gennaro of course – are uploading exclusive videos every week, with plenty of clever tips, tricks and methods that'll help transform your cooking.

When I first started this series of books, my ambition was to launch new talent, but with Gennaro, this isn't quite the case – he's already published many successful books and broadcast great TV shows. But nevertheless, with just a couple of Food Tube years under his belt, he is new to the digital world. His talent and passion had never been in question, but I wondered if he could smash it on this new online platform (before he came on board, I don't think he even knew what YouTube was!). And the answer is a massive resounding yes! Gennaro's energy and enthusiasm on camera – showing us how to cook incredible Italian food – has inspired the Food Tube community in a big way, he really is second to none.

So, enjoy this pocket-sized cookbook, full of incredible, achievable pasta recipes, from the very basics to kick-ass dishes for any night of the week. Buon appetito!

youtube.com/jamieoliver

HELLO LOVELY PEOPLE!

I'm so excited to introduce you to my first Food Tube book, where I've dedicated a whole 50 recipes to Italy's favourite food and, of course, mine too – pasta!

Pasta is an essential part of the Italian diet and a lot of traditional families serve it at least once a day. From its humble origins of mammas and nonnas at home mixing flour and water or flour and egg yolks, it's become a worldwide industry. It turns out that it's not just the Italians who love it.

The beauty of pasta is that it's quick, simple and versatile – from easy tomato sauces to toss through spaghetti, to slow-cooked ragùs and warming baked dishes – you can make pasta as rich or as light as you like, depending on the seasons and your budget. I was brought up eating and cooking with fresh, seasonal produce, which is why I've split my recipes according to the seasons – if you follow this philosophy, you'll find your cooking benefits all the more for it.

Being Italian, pasta has always been a big part of my life. As a child I often watched my mother make fresh pasta, which was always the eggless variety, typical of southern Italy – she never used a pasta machine, just her good old rolling pin. My mamma would make it at least once a week, usually on Sundays to go with my aunt's slow-cooked meat ragù, which would've bubbled on the stove for hours and hours, or even overnight. I still can't recreate that incredible taste, even now.

Of course, we also ate dried pasta and this was our main staple during the week. Like most Italians, we kept a good selection in our store cupboard – some long pasta shapes, such as spaghetti and linguine, some short, such as penne and rigatoni, some shapes for baking, such as lasagne sheets and conchiglioni, and some small shapes to add to soups. In Italy, you can find more than 600 different pasta shapes, but even I haven't tried them all yet. In this book, I've included plenty of varieties, so you can be adventurous and try something new or rely on your old favourites.

So, lovely people, I hope you love these fantastic recipes. Make sure you watch my videos on Food Tube for plenty more of my pasta recipes and ideas. Tune in, keep cooking and enjoy!

✳✳✳
CONTENTS

⇒ BASICS ⇐

ꝑꝑꝑꝑ SPRING ꝑꝑꝑꝑ

SUMMER

AUTUMN

WINTER

MY TOP TIPS

INGREDIENTS

Always use Tipo 00 flour when making pasta because it's finer than other varieties and easier to work with. Fine semolina is also a must – it has a good, coarse texture that helps to give the dough a lovely lift and lightness.

When making egg pasta, always use large free-range or organic eggs – it makes all the difference! They don't have to be chicken eggs either; try duck eggs for a richer flavour, or experiment with quail and guinea fowl eggs too.

ROLLING PASTA

Keep plenty of fine semolina to hand when rolling pasta – it helps to stop the pasta sticking together as you work.

Always wrap pasta dough in clingfilm and cover rolled pasta sheets with a damp tea towel to stop them drying out when you're busy with something else.

COOKING PASTA

Adding salt to the pasta water is very important. I use 10g of sea salt to every 3 litres of water. That might sound like a lot, but the pasta doesn't absorb it all. This amount will simply lick the pasta and give it a nice flavour.

You need lots of boiling water in a big pan so the pasta can dance about. A pan that's too small will suffocate it. The water should be at a rolling boil before you add the pasta, to avoid gloopy, limp results.

Always remember to save a cupful of cooking water before draining your pasta. It acts like a flavoured broth, loosening the sauce and helping to coat the pasta and make it nice and glossy.

We Italians always cook pasta until it's very slightly undercooked, or 'al dente' as we like to say. This translates as 'to the tooth', because it should be soft enough to eat but still with a bit of bite. Cooking pasta this way is best as it takes longer to chew, giving you more time to properly taste and digest it. Fresh pasta can take anywhere between 1 and 6 minutes to cook – use your head and keep checking it. There is nothing worse than over-cooked pasta!

TIME TO ENJOY

Italians have certain rules about which pasta shape goes with which sauce – there are lots of exceptions of course, but try to keep long pasta shapes, like linguine, with quick, light sauces and short shapes, like penne, with heavier, robust sauces and ragùs.

USEFUL EQUIPMENT

3

My **WOODEN BUTTER PAT** is a great piece of equipment when making pasta shapes like gnocchetti and garganelli. To keep it from sliding about on your work surface, simply flatten a piece of dough underneath it to stick it in place.

1

PASTA MACHINES are a great investment – they will cut your work in half. Make sure you spend a bit of money on a quality, hard-wearing one – you don't want it falling apart in a few years! When you've finished using it, rub it with a leftover lump of pasta dough so it's nice and clean for next time.

4

It's important to have a **PASTRY BRUSH** when working with filled fresh pasta, like ravioli or rotolo. I'm well practised and can work quickly, but if it takes you a little longer, brush your pasta sheets with a little water to stop them drying out. Keep old pastry brushes and use them to get the hard-to-reach bits out of your pasta machine when you're done.

2

You can, of course, roll out pasta using a **ROLLING PIN** – my mother and all the nonnas before her did, but you have to be far more precise and it's hard work!

5

When it comes to **PASTRY CUTTERS**, it's good to have plenty of different shapes and sizes. The square and round cutters can help you create more precise shapes, while the single wheel cutters will neaten up any rough edges.

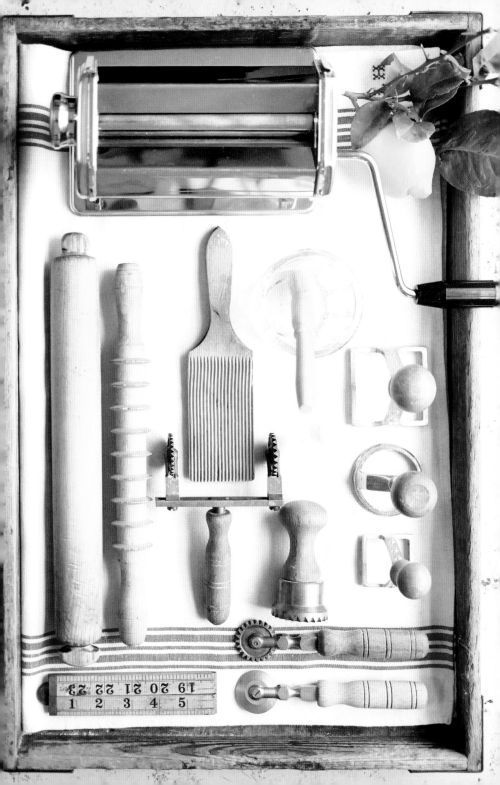

BASICS

A few basics and all the old classics.

PASTA DOUGH

150g Tipo 00 flour,
plus extra for dusting

50g fine semolina

2 large free-range eggs

Combine the flour and semolina on a clean work surface or in a large bowl. Make a well in the middle and break in the eggs. With a fork or using your hands, gradually mix the flour with the eggs until it's all mixed together. Lightly dust a board or work surface with flour, then knead the dough by stretching it out with the palm of your hand, rolling it back, then stretching it out again. Keep stretching and rolling it until you get a smooth, soft dough. Pat into a ball, wrap in clingfilm and leave to rest for at least 30 minutes, or until needed.

Egg pasta dough is more common in the north of Italy for shapes such as tagliatelle and lasagne, or filled pasta like ravioli. When you go further south, **eggless pasta dough** is used a lot more, as historically people there had less money to buy eggs. To go eggless, gradually pour 80ml of lukewarm water into the well instead, mixing as you go. Eggless pasta cooks quickly, so be careful not to overdo it. This is my recipe, but I'm sure there are five million Italian mammas each with their own method.

If you want to make this for more people, simply increase the amounts using the ratio of 100g of flour to 1 large egg or, for eggless pasta, 100g of flour to 40ml of water. For how to turn your dough into different shapes, see pages 18 to 20.

UNFILLED PASTA SHAPES

To make **orecchiette** or **gnocchetti**, roll the **pasta dough** (see page 16) into a 2cm-thick sausage shape. For orecchiette, cut off a 1cm piece of pasta, then carefully pull the edge of the knife along the dough to flatten it out, holding an edge with your finger to keep it in place. Mould it around your thumb to create an orecchietta, or in English, 'little ear'. For gnocchetti, cut off a 2cm piece of dough and place on a wooden butter pat. Gently press the flat side of a knife on top, then carefully pull it towards you so the dough rolls into a ridged shell-like shape. For **fusilli**, roll the dough with your hands until it's about the thickness of a pencil, then cut it into 5cm lengths. Press and roll each length around a metal skewer, pull the skewer out and you have fusilli!

For the following shapes, flatten a ball of pasta dough, about the size of a big orange, with your hands, then roll through a pasta machine at the widest setting. Continue to roll the pasta through the machine, turning down the settings as you go, until you get to number 1 and your dough is wafer thin. Trim the pasta sheet to get rid of any uneven edges.

For **farfalle**, cut the pasta sheet into little rectangles (you decide how big you want them), then pinch each of the longest sides together into a butterfly shape. To make **garganelli**, cut the pasta sheet into 3cm squares and place one at a time on a wooden butter pat. Starting at one corner roll it around the handle of a wooden spoon to the opposite corner, gently pressing into the pat as you do so, then pull out the handle. To make **straccetti**, or 'little rips', tear the pasta sheet or any leftover strips into rough pieces, any size you like. Easy!

Turn pasta into **pappardelle**, **tagliatelle** or **taglierini** by loosely rolling up the pasta sheet. Slice the rolled-up pasta to your desired thickness: about 2½cm thick for pappardelle, 1cm thick for tagliatelle and 3mm thick for taglierini. And finally, for **lasagne sheets**, cut the pasta sheet into 12cm x 18cm rectangles (this much pasta will make about 10 sheets). You can also turn these into **cannelloni**: blanch the lasagne sheets for about 30 seconds, pipe the filling along one side and brush the other side with water. Roll up and press to seal.

To stop your pasta sticking, keep lightly dusting it with semolina as you work. For more help, and to watch me making some of these shapes, go to youtube.com/jamieoliver.

FILLED PASTA SHAPES

Start by dusting your work surface with flour and make sure you have lots of room! Flatten a ball of **pasta dough** (see page 16), about the size of a big orange, with your hands, then roll through a pasta machine at the widest setting. Continue to roll the pasta through the machine, turning down the settings as you go, until you get to number 1 and your dough is almost wafer-thin (filled pasta is usually slightly thicker than the unfilled types).

This is a rough guide – you can make your filled pasta bigger or smaller, just adjust the amount of filling you use accordingly. There are no rules!

– RAVIOLI –

This is the most classic pasta shape and probably the easiest one to fill. Trim the pasta sheet so you have a large rectangle, then brush all over with a little water. Roll heaped tablespoons of the filling into balls, then place them in a row along the centre of the pasta sheet at 7cm intervals. Take one of the longest pasta edges, fold it over the filling, and bring the two edges together. Use your hands to press gently around the balls of filling, squeezing out any air. Cut into 7cm squares to seal – I like to use a serrated pasta cutter.

– CAPPELLACCI –

Cut the pasta sheet into 8cm squares – I like to use a serrated pasta cutter. Roll teaspoons of the filling into balls and place one in the middle of each square. Fold one corner over the filling to form a filled triangle, then press the edges together, squeezing out any air. Roll the filled section of pasta away from you onto the far corner, then pull in the two remaining corners and press one on top of the other to seal.

– MEZZELUNE & TORTELLINI –

Cut the pasta sheet into 6cm rounds – I like to use a serrated circular pasta cutter. Roll ½ teaspoons of the filling into balls and place one in the middle of each round. Fold each round into a half-moon shape, then press the edges together, squeezing out any air. This is the classic mezzelune shape, but if you want tortellini, roll the filled section of pasta away from you onto the far edge, then pull back the two remaining corners and press one on top of the other to seal.

SIMPLE TOMATO SAUCE

SERVES 6-8

TOTAL TIME: 40 MINUTES

Tip **4 x 400g tins of plum tomatoes** into a bowl, then break them up with your hands. Pour in **1 tin of cold water**. Peel and finely slice **3 cloves of garlic** and ½ **a fresh red chilli (optional)**, then pick and roughly chop the leaves from **1 bunch of fresh basil**. Put the garlic, chilli and **4 tablespoons of extra virgin olive oil** into a large pan over a high heat. Cook for 2 minutes, then add the tomatoes and basil leaves. Season with **sea salt and freshly ground black pepper**, bring to the boil, then reduce the heat to low. Cook for 30 minutes, or until thickened to a rich, silky sauce. Serve with your favourite pasta or my **spinach & ricotta rotolo** (see page 58). To make passata, pass the sauce through a sieve, pushing through all those lovely juices with the base of a ladle.

OVEN-BAKED TOMATO SAUCE

SERVES 4

TOTAL TIME: 25 MINUTES

Preheat the oven to 220°C/425°F/gas 7. Place a large roasting tray in the oven to get hot. Meanwhile, quarter **650g of ripe vine cherry tomatoes** and place in a bowl. Peel and chop **4 cloves of garlic** and chop **1 fresh red chilli**, then add to the bowl. Pick in the leaves from **1 bunch of fresh basil**, add **6 tablespoons of extra virgin olive oil** and a good pinch of **sea salt** and mix well with your hands. Tip into the hot tray and return to the oven for 10 to 15 minutes, or until golden and softened. Serve with spaghetti and **a grating of Parmesan cheese**. Alternatively, I sometimes like to keep this sauce raw and serve it with orecchiette, a little more oil and a grating of Parmesan.

TRADITIONAL BASIL PESTO

SERVES 4

TOTAL TIME: 10 MINUTES

1 clove of garlic, peeled

1 pinch of sea salt

40g fresh basil leaves

15g pine nuts

50g Parmesan cheese

30g pecorino cheese

80ml extra virgin olive oil

If you're making this in a pestle and mortar, put in the garlic and salt and pound to a rough paste. Add the basil leaves and continue pounding it down, then add the pine nuts and finely grate in the cheeses. Continue pounding the mixture until you get a paste. Gradually drizzle in the oil, mixing it in until combined.

If you're making this in a food processor or blender, pulse the garlic and salt together a few times to a rough paste. Add the basil leaves and pulse again, then add the pine nuts and finely grate in the cheeses. Continue pulsing until you get a paste, but don't overdo it – the heat of the machine may turn the pesto bitter. Gradually add the oil, pulsing as you go until just combined.

Serve the pesto immediately with freshly cooked pasta, or place in an airtight jar and cover with a little oil so it doesn't dry up. Store in the fridge for up to 4 weeks until needed.

Traditionally, pesto is made in a pestle and mortar and that's how I like it – with a bit of crunch. As I'm from Amalfi, I love lemons! Sometimes I add a squeeze of juice right at the end of the recipe, but see what you're in the mood for.

SIMPLE BUTTER & SAGE SAUCE

TOTAL TIME: 5 MINUTES

100g unsalted butter

8 fresh sage leaves

70ml hot organic vegetable stock

40g Parmesan cheese,
plus extra to serve

Place the butter and sage leaves in a large frying pan over a medium heat. Allow the butter to melt, then add the hot stock and finely grate in the Parmesan. Tip in your chosen drained pasta and toss well over the heat until you get a beautifully creamy, rich sauce, then serve immediately with an extra grating of Parmesan. If you're using filled pasta, be gentle, as they can be quite delicate. To see how to make **cappellacci** (as pictured here), see page 20.

The traditional recipe burns the butter, but I prefer to add stock – it infuses with the butter and sage to create a lovely, rich, creamy sauce. You will love it!

26

CLASSIC SPAGHETTI CARBONARA

SERVES 2

TOTAL TIME: 10 MINUTES

3 large free-range egg yolks

40g Parmesan cheese,
plus extra to serve

sea salt and freshly ground
black pepper

1 x 150g piece of
higher-welfare pancetta

200g spaghetti

1 clove of garlic, peeled

extra virgin olive oil

Put the egg yolks into a bowl, finely grate in the Parmesan, season with pepper, then mix well with a fork and put to one side. Cut any hard skin off the pancetta and set aside, then chop the meat.

Cook the spaghetti in a large pan of boiling salted water until al dente. Meanwhile, rub the pancetta skin, if you have any, all over the base of a medium frying pan (this will add fantastic flavour, or use 1 tablespoon of oil instead), then place over a medium-high heat. Crush the garlic clove with the palm of your hand, add it to the pan and leave it to flavour the fat for a minute. Stir in the pancetta, then cook for 4 minutes, or until it starts to crisp up.

Pick out and discard the garlic from the pan, then, reserving some of the cooking water, drain and add the spaghetti. Toss well over the heat so it really soaks up all that lovely flavour, then remove the pan from the heat. Add a splash of the cooking water and toss well, season with pepper, then pour in the egg mixture – the pan will help to cook the egg gently, rather than scrambling it. Toss well, adding more cooking water until it's lovely and glossy. Serve with a grating of Parmesan and an extra twist of pepper.

Use ready-sliced quality pancetta if you can't buy it in one piece. It's traditional to use spaghetti in this recipe, but bucatini or rigatoni are just as good.

BOLOGNESE RAGÙ
WITH TAGLIATELLE

SERVES 4

TOTAL TIME: 2 HOURS 30 MINUTES

extra virgin olive oil

250g beef mince

250g higher-welfare pork mince

1 sprig of fresh rosemary

1 onion, peeled

1 stick of celery, trimmed

1 carrot, trimmed

150ml quality red wine

2 tablespoons tomato purée

1 litre hot organic beef or vegetable stock

400g tagliatelle (if making fresh, see pages 16 & 18)

sea salt and freshly ground black pepper

Parmesan cheese, to serve

Heat 3 tablespoons of oil in a large pan over a high heat. Add all the mince and cook for 5 to 10 minutes, or until lightly browned all over, continuously stirring and breaking it up with the back of a spoon. Stir in the rosemary sprig to add great flavour, then cook for a further 5 to 10 minutes, or until the liquid has evaporated and the meat is a dark golden colour – you must wait for it to deepen in colour; it's the secret to a really good Bolognese.

Meanwhile, finely chop the onion, celery and carrot. Pour the wine into the pan and let it bubble away. Stir in the chopped vegetables, cook for a minute or two so the flavours really mix, then add the tomato purée. Stir well for a minute, pour in the hot stock, then simmer over a low heat for 1 hour 30 minutes to 2 hours, or until thickened and reduced.

When the ragù is nearly ready, cook the tagliatelle in a large pan of boiling salted water until al dente. Season the ragù to taste with salt and pepper and remove the rosemary sprig. Reserving some of the cooking water, drain the pasta and add to the ragù. Toss well over the heat until lovely and glossy, adding a splash of the cooking water, if needed. Serve with a grating of Parmesan.

I was fortunate to learn how to make a proper Bolognese in Bologna when I was only 20 years old. There are no chopped tomatoes in the original – you don't need them, this recipe gives you a lovely, rich, sweet flavour.

MIDNIGHT SPAGHETTATA

SERVES
2

TOTAL TIME: 10 MINUTES

200g spaghetti

sea salt and freshly ground
black pepper

3 cloves of garlic, peeled

1 fresh red chilli

½ a bunch of fresh flat-leaf parsley,
leaves picked

extra virgin olive oil

Parmesan cheese, to serve

This is a quick and simple dish that we Italians love to cook after an evening out, when we're hungry but the fridge is empty. Cook the spaghetti in a large pan of boiling salted water until al dente.

Meanwhile, finely slice the garlic and chilli, then roughly chop the parsley leaves. Heat 4 tablespoons of oil in a large frying pan over a medium-high heat, then add the garlic and chilli. Sweat for 3 to 4 minutes, or until turning golden. Reserving some of the cooking water, drain and add the spaghetti to the pan. Toss well over the heat until lovely and glossy, adding a splash of the cooking water to loosen, if needed. Stir in the parsley leaves, then serve with a grating of Parmesan and a twist of pepper.

When I cook with fresh chilli, I always give it a smell to see how flavourful it is. You want a good, strong chilli flavour here, so use more if you think it needs it.

PASTA FRITTATA
LOTS OF WAYS

SERVES
4

TOTAL TIME: 20 MINUTES

FOR BASIC PASTA FRITTATA

4 large free-range eggs

40g Parmesan cheese,
plus extra to serve

sea salt and freshly ground
black pepper

400g leftover cooked pasta

extra virgin olive oil

Pasta frittata is delicious
served hot or cold – I like
to wrap it up to have as a
snack during a long walk
or a day out foraging in
the woods or, take it out
for a picnic.

Preheat the oven to 200°C/400°F/gas 6. Beat the eggs in a large bowl, then finely grate in the Parmesan. Season with a little salt and a good twist of pepper. Whisk well, then stir in your pasta.

To cook the frittata, heat 3 tablespoons of oil in a 26cm non-stick ovenproof frying pan over a medium heat. Add the frittata mixture and cook for about 5 minutes, or until crisp underneath, then place in the oven for another 5 minutes, or until firm. Carefully flip the frittata onto a large plate, then slide it back into the pan and return it to the oven for a further 5 minutes, or until crisp underneath. Serve with an extra grating of Parmesan.

If you've got about 400g of leftover cooked pasta which is already coated in sauce, you can swap that in for an easy twist on my basic recipe. Or try making a pizzaiola pasta frittata – make the basic pasta frittata (I like to use fusilli, but use whatever shape you have), then serve by slicing and layering over **6 ripe cherry tomatoes** and **40g of fontina cheese**. Scatter over **a few fresh basil leaves**, and finish with an extra grating of Parmesan.

If it's springtime, make the basic recipe extra special by adding peas and pancetta. Heat **1½ tablespoons of extra virgin olive oil** in a 26cm non-stick ovenproof frying pan. Peel, finely slice and add **1 onion**, then sweat for a few minutes. Very finely slice **6 higher-welfare slices of pancetta** and add to the pan for a further 2 to 3 minutes. Stir in **200g of peas**, pour in 400ml of hot water, then turn the heat up to high and bring to the boil. Leave it to simmer for 10 to 15 minutes, or until the liquid has evaporated, then cool. Make the basic pasta frittata mixture, finely chop and add the leaves from **4 sprigs of fresh mint**, squeeze in the juice from **1 lemon**, then stir in the cooled pea mixture. Cook your frittata as above, and serve with an extra grating of Parmesan.

SPRING

Spring is the time to celebrate the first herbs and vegetables of the season. Fresh peas, broad beans, asparagus, courgettes and spinach are all perfect for lovely light pasta sauces. It's also the best season to forage for nettles, sorrel, rocket and wild garlic.

SPRING VEGETABLE RAGÙ
WITH PENNE

SERVES
6

TOTAL TIME: 1 HOUR
30 MINUTES

1 shallot, peeled

1 stick of celery, 1 carrot,
1 small courgette and
1 small fennel bulb, trimmed

200g asparagus

1 bunch of fresh flat-leaf parsley,
leaves picked and stalks reserved

1 bunch of fresh basil,
leaves picked and stalks reserved

2 baby artichokes

juice from 1 lemon

extra virgin olive oil

200g fresh peas, shelled

200g fresh broad beans,
podded and shelled

2 x 400g tins of chopped tomatoes

800ml hot organic vegetable stock

sea salt and freshly ground
black pepper

50g baby spinach

600g penne

Parmesan cheese, to serve

Start by preparing your vegetables. Finely dice the shallot, celery, carrot, courgette and fennel (reserving any fennel fronds). Use a vegetable peeler to shave any tough stringy bits from the asparagus stalks, then slice off the woody ends and discard. Finely slice the stalks, reserving the tips for later, then finely slice the parsley and basil stalks.

Next, prepare the artichokes. Fill a bowl with cold water and the lemon juice – the acidity will stop the artichokes from discolouring. Using a sharp knife, cut away and discard the stalk from one of the artichokes about 2½cm below the base. Chop off and peel the remaining stalk with your knife until you get to the sweeter inner core, then add it to the bowl. Start pulling, breaking off and discarding the leaves until you get to the pale, thinner leaves. Cut off and discard the top part of the artichoke so you're left with the pale base, then trim away any scruffy bits. Halve lengthways and add to the water while you prepare the remaining artichoke. Once finished, open out each artichoke like a flower, scoop out the fluffy core with a teaspoon and discard, then finely slice lengthways.

Heat 6 tablespoons of oil in a large, wide pan over a medium-high heat, then add the chopped vegetables and herb stalks, peas and broad beans. Sweat for 5 to 10 minutes, then pour in the tomatoes and hot stock, bring to the boil and season with salt and pepper. Stir in the spinach and reserved asparagus tips, then simmer over a low heat for 45 minutes, or until thickened and reduced.

When there's 10 minutes to go, cook the penne in a large pan of boiling salted water until al dente. Reserving some of the cooking water, drain the penne and add to the sauce. Toss well over the heat until lovely and glossy, adding a splash of the cooking water to loosen, if needed. Sprinkle over any reserved fennel fronds, some parsley and basil leaves, then serve with a grating of Parmesan.

WILD ROCKET & PECORINO ORECCHIETTE

 SERVES 4

TOTAL TIME: 20 MINUTES

2 cloves of garlic, peeled

2 sticks of celery, trimmed

½ a fresh red chilli

8 spring onions, trimmed

2 large firm tomatoes

400g orecchiette
(if making fresh, see pages 16 & 18)

sea salt and freshly ground
black pepper

extra virgin olive oil

6 anchovy fillets

juice from ½ a lemon

100g wild rocket, washed

pecorino cheese, to serve

Start by preparing your ingredients. Finely slice the garlic, celery, chilli and spring onions. Quarter the tomatoes and cut out the seeds, then dice the flesh.

Cook the orecchiette in a large pan of boiling salted water until al dente. Meanwhile, heat 5 tablespoons of oil in a large frying pan over a medium heat. Add the garlic, celery and whole anchovies and fry for 30 seconds, then stir in the chilli and spring onions. Sweat for a few minutes, or until just starting to soften – you want to keep the sauce quite raw so the onions retain their fresh flavour.

Reserving some of the cooking water, drain the orecchiette and add to the sauce. Toss well over the heat until lovely and glossy, adding a splash of the cooking water to loosen, if needed. Season carefully with salt, add the lemon juice, then remove from the heat. Toss in the tomatoes and rocket, then serve with shavings of pecorino, a drizzle of oil and a twist of pepper, if you like.

> With lemons, fresh tomatoes, wild rocket and anchovies that smell like the sea, this is a classic recipe from my hometown of Minori. You can exchange the orecchiette for other short pasta shapes, if you like.

RICOTTA, LEMON & MINT CULURZONES

 SERVES 4

TOTAL TIME: 1 HOUR
PLUS RESTING

sea salt

1 x **pasta dough** (see page 16)

FOR THE FILLING

3 sprigs of fresh mint, leaves picked

200g quality ricotta cheese
(available at Italian delis)

1 large free-range egg yolk

2½ unwaxed lemons

30g Parmesan cheese,
plus extra to serve

FOR THE SAUCE

200g unsalted butter, cubed

8 sprigs of fresh mint,
leaves picked

200ml hot organic vegetable stock

To make the filling, finely chop the mint leaves, then put them into a bowl with the ricotta, egg yolk and zest from 1½ lemons. Squeeze in the juice from ½ a lemon, then finely grate in the Parmesan and season with salt. Scrunch the mixture together with your hands until combined (it needs to be quite firm).

To roll the pasta, dust your work surface with flour (make sure you have lots of room!). Divide the **pasta dough** into four portions, flatten each with your hands, then roll through a pasta machine at the widest setting. Continue to roll the pasta through the machine, turning down the settings as you go, until you get to number 1 and your dough is almost wafer thin (cover the rolled sheets with a damp tea towel). Cut each sheet into 10cm squares, then place 1 teaspoon of the filling at one corner of each square. Keeping the filling in place with your thumb, fold up that corner so it just covers the filling, then fold over the dough from the right side, pushing it against your nail to make a pleat, then repeat from the left. Continue until the dough covers the filling and you've created a plaited shape, like you see in the pictures. Pinch the dough just above the filling to seal. Repeat until you have 16 in total.

Make the sauce by putting the butter, mint leaves, hot stock and the juice from the remaining 2 lemons into a large frying pan over a medium heat. Season lightly with salt, then cook for about 12 minutes, or until reduced by half. Meanwhile, cook the culurzones in a large pan of boiling salted water until they rise to the surface, then use a slotted spoon to transfer them to the sauce. Toss well over the heat for a minute until nicely coated, then add a good grating of Parmesan and divide between your plates. Serve with an extra grating of Parmesan and lemon zest, if you like.

Sardinian culurzones are a tricky shape to master, but you can use this filling in any other filled pasta shape if you want something a little easier (see page 20).

PARMA HAM & ASPARAGUS
WITH GIGLI

SERVES
4

TOTAL TIME: 25 MINUTES

90g higher-welfare slices
of Parma ham

1 onion, peeled

600g asparagus

extra virgin olive oil

400g gigli

sea salt and freshly ground
black pepper

400ml hot organic vegetable stock

20g Parmesan cheese,
plus extra to serve

juice from ½ a lemon

Start by preparing your ingredients. Slice the Parma ham into strips and finely chop the onion. Use a vegetable peeler to shave any tough stringy bits from the asparagus stalks, then slice off the woody ends and discard. Finely slice the stalks, reserving the tips.

Put the Parma ham into a large dry frying pan over a medium-high heat and cook for 5 minutes, or until crispy. Add 3 tablespoons of oil to the pan, then add the onion and sweat for 2 to 3 minutes to soften slightly, stirring often. Meanwhile, cook the gigli in a large pan of boiling salted water until very al dente – it'll continue cooking in the sauce, so it's important to undercook it. Add the asparagus stalks to the frying pan, then after 2 minutes pour in the hot stock. Leave to simmer for 5 minutes, stirring in the asparagus tips for the final minute or so.

Reserving some of the cooking water, drain the gigli and add to the sauce. Stir gently over the heat, adding a splash of the cooking water to loosen, if needed, then cook for a further few minutes to let the pasta soak up all those lovely flavours. Season carefully to taste with salt and pepper, grate in the Parmesan, add a squeeze of lemon juice, stir well, then serve with an extra grating of Parmesan.

Gigli means 'daffodils' in Italian, thanks to their beautiful, flower-like shape. If you can't find gigli, castellane or farfalle work just as well.

FRESH BROAD BEAN & MINT
WITH DITALINI

100g higher-welfare slices
of pancetta

1 bunch of spring onions, trimmed

300g fresh broad beans,
podded and shells left on

400g ditalini

sea salt

extra virgin olive oil

200ml hot organic vegetable stock

4 sprigs of fresh mint, leaves picked

juice from ½ a lemon

20g pecorino cheese,
plus extra to serve

Start by preparing your ingredients. Finely slice the pancetta and spring onions. Skin any larger broad beans as the shells are generally quite tough, leaving the small ones intact.

Cook the ditalini in a large pan of boiling salted water until very al dente – it'll continue cooking in the sauce, so it's important to undercook it. Meanwhile, heat 3 tablespoons of oil in a large frying pan over a medium heat. Add the pancetta and cook for 2 to 3 minutes, or until starting to crisp up, then stir in the spring onions and sweat for about 30 seconds. Add the broad beans and pour in the hot stock. Cook for just 2 minutes, or until the beans have softened slightly.

Reserving some of the cooking water, drain the ditalini and add to the pan. Stir gently, adding a splash of the cooking water to loosen, if needed, then cook for a further few minutes to let the ditalini soak up all those lovely flavours. Very finely slice the mint leaves, then stir most of them into the pan (they will add a beautiful freshness). Add a squeeze of lemon juice, finely grate in the pecorino and stir well. Serve with a drizzle of oil, an extra grating of pecorino and the rest of the chopped mint leaves – fantastic!

If you can't find ditalini, use penne instead.

TROUT CAVATELLI

SERVES 4

TOTAL TIME: 30 MINUTES

3 x 400g trout fillets, skin on, scaled and pin-boned

2 firm tomatoes

2 cloves of garlic, peeled

½ a fresh red chilli

5 anchovy fillets

1 bunch of spring onions, trimmed

3 higher-welfare slices of pancetta

1 handful of wild fennel herbs

400g cavatelli

sea salt and freshly ground black pepper

extra virgin olive oil

½ tablespoon baby capers, rinsed

60ml quality white wine

juice from ½ a lemon

Start by preparing your ingredients. Slice the trout into 3cm strips. Halve the tomatoes and cut out the seeds, then roughly chop the flesh. Finely chop the garlic, chilli, anchovies, spring onions and pancetta (keeping the spring onions and pancetta separate). Remove any tough stalky bits from the fennel.

Cook the cavatelli in a large pan of boiling salted water until al dente. Meanwhile, heat 5 tablespoons of oil in a large frying pan over a medium heat, then add the garlic, chilli, anchovies and capers. Sweat for a minute or so, then add the spring onions and cook for a further minute to soften slightly. Stir in the pancetta and trout, then season lightly with salt. Cook for 5 minutes, or until the fish is just cooked through.

Pour in the wine and let it bubble away, then, reserving some of the cooking water, drain the cavatelli and add to the pan. Toss well over the heat until lovely and glossy, adding a splash of the cooking water to loosen, if needed. Stir in the tomatoes, fennel and lemon juice. Serve with a drizzle of oil and a twist of pepper.

Wild fennel grows everywhere in the spring. For the best results and maximum flavour, pick it yourself, otherwise the bushy fronds of a regular fennel bulb will do. If you can't find cavatelli, use casarecce or linguine instead.

COURGETTE FLOWERS, PRAWNS & LEMON
WITH LINGUINE

4 anchovy fillets

1 shallot, peeled

¼ of a fresh red chilli

2 cloves of garlic, peeled

8 baby courgettes, trimmed

400g linguine

sea salt

extra virgin olive oil

200g small peeled cooked prawns

1 splash of quality white wine

10 whole courgette flowers

½ a bunch of fresh basil,
leaves picked

juice from 1 lemon

Start by preparing your ingredients. Finely slice the anchovies, shallot, chilli and garlic. Slice the courgettes lengthways, then thinly slice them at an angle.

Cook the linguine in a large pan of boiling salted water until al dente. Meanwhile, heat 4 tablespoons of oil in a large frying pan over a medium-high heat, then add the anchovies and cook for 1 minute, or until they dissolve. Add the shallot, chilli and garlic and sweat for a few minutes, or until starting to soften. Stir in the prawns, cook for a minute, then pour in the wine and let it bubble away. Add the courgettes and cook for 3 minutes, or until tender.

Reserving some of the cooking water, drain the linguine and add to the pan. Season carefully with salt, then toss well over the heat until lovely and glossy, adding a splash of the cooking water to loosen, if needed. Remove from the heat, tear in the courgette flowers and most of the basil leaves, and add the lemon juice (I add a splash of anchovy oil from the jar, too). Serve with a drizzle of extra virgin olive oil and the reserved basil leaves.

Baby courgettes are the first courgettes of the year,
so this dish is perfect for spring. If you only have
the regular variety, add them to the pan slightly
earlier so they get a chance to cook properly.

ARTICHOKE & RICOTTA SEDANINI

SERVES 4

TOTAL TIME: 40 MINUTES

5 baby artichokes

juice from 1 lemon

400g sedanini

sea salt and freshly ground
black pepper

2 shallots, peeled

extra virgin olive oil

1 pinch of dried red chilli flakes

200ml hot organic vegetable stock

150g quality ricotta cheese
(available at Italian delis)

50g Parmesan cheese,
plus extra to serve

½ a bunch of fresh flat-leaf parsley,
leaves picked

This recipe comes from the Sicilian village of Certa, which is famous for its artichokes. If you love artichokes as much as I do, this recipe is definitely for you. The ricotta gives it a lovely creaminess too.

Start by preparing the artichokes. Fill a bowl with cold water and the lemon juice – the acidity will stop the artichokes from discolouring. Using a sharp knife, cut away and discard the stalk from one of the artichokes about 2½cm below the base. Chop off and peel the remaining stalk with your knife until you get to the sweeter inner core, then add it to the bowl. Start pulling, breaking off and discarding the leaves until you get to the pale, thinner leaves. Cut off and discard the top part of the artichoke so you're left with the pale base, then trim away any scruffy bits. Halve lengthways and add to the water while you prepare the remaining artichokes. When you're finished, open out each artichoke like a flower, scoop out the fluffy core with a teaspoon and discard, then return them to the water.

Cook the sedanini in a large pan of boiling salted water until al dente. Meanwhile, finely slice the artichokes lengthways and finely slice the shallots. Put the shallots into a large frying pan with 2 tablespoons of oil and sweat for 2 minutes over a medium-high heat, or until softened. Add the artichokes and chilli flakes, fry for a further 2 to 3 minutes, or until turning golden, then pour in the hot stock and simmer until just tender. Stir in the ricotta and a twist of pepper and cook until deliciously creamy, stirring often.

Reserving some of the cooking water, drain the sedanini and add to the sauce. Toss well over the heat until lovely and glossy, adding a splash of the cooking water to loosen, if needed. Finely grate in the Parmesan, finely slice and stir in most of the parsley leaves, then season to taste with salt and pepper. Serve with a grating of Parmesan and the reserved parsley leaves.

BASIL PESTO & RED MULLET
WITH TAGLIATELLE

TOTAL TIME: 30 MINUTES

2 medium potatoes, peeled

200g green beans, trimmed

4 x 100g red mullet fillets, skin on,
scaled and pin-boned

extra virgin olive oil

sea salt and freshly ground
black pepper

400g tagliatelle
(if making fresh, see pages 16 & 18)

4 tablespoons **traditional basil
pesto** (see page 24)

Start by preparing your ingredients. Halve the potatoes, then slice into thin wedges. Cut the green beans in half. Wash the red mullet under cold running water, then pat dry with kitchen paper. Heat 3 tablespoons of oil in a large frying pan over a medium-high heat, add the fish and season lightly with salt. Cook for 2 minutes on each side, or until golden and crisp.

Meanwhile, put the potatoes and green beans into a large pan of boiling salted water over a high heat. Bring back to the boil, then add the tagliatelle (if you're using fresh, only add it for the final few minutes). Cook for about 8 minutes, or until the pasta is al dente and the vegetables are tender.

Once cooked, remove the fish to a board and slice at an angle into chunks. Put the **traditional basil pesto** into a large bowl. Reserving some of the cooking water, drain the tagliatelle and vegetables and add to the bowl. Toss well, adding a splash of the cooking water to loosen, if needed, then season carefully to taste with salt and pepper. Serve immediately, topped with the red mullet.

Never add pesto to a hot pan because it will ruin its delicate flavour – when coating pasta, tip it into a bowl before combining it with the pesto.

SPINACH & RICOTTA ROTOLO
WITH SIMPLE TOMATO SAUCE

TOTAL TIME: 2 HOURS
PLUS RESTING

1 x **pasta dough** (see page 16)

1 large free-range egg, beaten

½ x **simple tomato sauce**
(see page 22)

FOR THE FILLING

6 banana shallots, peeled

extra virgin olive oil

300g spinach, washed

sea salt and freshly ground
black pepper

50g Parmesan cheese,
plus extra for grating

¼ of a whole nutmeg

2 large free-range eggs

400g quality ricotta cheese
(available at Italian delis)

1 x 125g ball of mozzarella cheese

For the filling, finely chop the shallots. Heat 2 tablespoons of oil in a large frying pan over a medium heat. Sweat the shallots for 10 minutes, or until soft. Add the spinach, season and wilt, then cool. Finely grate the Parmesan and nutmeg into a bowl, add the eggs and ricotta, season, then scrunch together. Squeeze the moisture out of the spinach, very finely chop it, and scrunch in.

To roll the pasta, dust your work surface with flour (make sure you have lots of room!). Divide the **pasta dough** into three portions, flatten each with your hands, then roll through a pasta machine at the widest setting. Continue to roll through the machine, turning down the settings as you go, until you get to number 1 and your dough is almost wafer thin (cover the rolled sheets with a damp tea towel). Working on a clean tea towel, trim the sheets to 45cm in length, then use beaten egg to stick the longest edges together, creating one large rectangle (about 35cm x 45cm).

Evenly spoon over the filling, leaving a 5cm border. Tear over the mozzarella, add a good grating of Parmesan, then brush the edges with beaten egg. Using the nearest edge of the tea towel, carefully roll it up, pressing the final edge to seal and folding up the ends. Roll up in the tea towel, twisting the ends like a Christmas cracker. Secure with string, then wrap tightly in clingfilm and secure with more string (see picture, page 56).

Put the rotolo into a deep roasting tray of boiling water over a high heat. Cook for 10 minutes, turning occasionally and topping up with more boiling water, if needed. Carefully unwrap, trim and discard the ends, then slice into 12 rounds. Serve with the **simple tomato sauce** and a grating of Parmesan. Alternatively, preheat the oven to 200°C/400°F/gas 6, place most of the simple tomato sauce in a large, wide ovenproof pan, and add the rotolo slices. Top each with more sauce and bake for 10 minutes, or until golden, grating over a little Parmesan just before the end.

SUMMER

Summer, for me, is all about long, lazy days by the sea, warm evening strolls (or 'passeggiate', as we say) and food al fresco with lots of grilled peppers, aubergines, fresh pasta salads and plenty of shellfish. At home in Italy, this is the season for preserving our beloved tomatoes, so that we have enough concentrated and sun-dried varieties to see us through the year.

PASTA SALAD
WITH GRILLED PEPPERS & OLIVES

SERVES
2

TOTAL TIME: 45 MINUTES

2 peppers,
mixed colours if possible

200g orecchiette
(if making fresh, see pages 16 & 18)

sea salt

1 firm tomato

12 black or green olives, stone in

2 sticks of celery, trimmed

½ a bunch of fresh flat-leaf parsley,
leaves picked

4 sprigs of fresh basil,
leaves picked

extra virgin olive oil

juice from 1 lemon

Place the whole peppers on a griddle pan over a high heat (or under the grill) for about 20 minutes, or until blackened all over. Remove to a bowl, cover with clingfilm and cool. Meanwhile, cook the orecchiette in a large pan of boiling salted water until al dente, then drain and refresh under cold water to stop it over-cooking.

Scrape the blackened skin away from the cooled peppers, then deseed and chop the flesh into 1cm chunks. Quarter the tomato, cut out the seeds and dice the flesh. Crush the olives with the palm of your hand, pull out and discard the stones, then tear in half. Finely slice the celery, then put it all into a large bowl. Roughly chop and add the parsley leaves and most of the basil leaves.

Add the orecchiette to the bowl with 4 tablespoons of oil and half the lemon juice. Toss well with your hands, then season to taste with salt and a squeeze more lemon juice, if needed. Serve with a drizzle of oil and a scattering of the reserved basil leaves.

Smoky peppers, crunchy celery, fresh lemon, olives and herbs, this is a taste of summer in your mouth.

PARMA HAM & RED PEPPER
WITH TAGLIERINI

TOTAL TIME: 20 MINUTES

½ a red or white onion, peeled

1 red pepper, deseeded

90g higher-welfare slices
of Parma ham

¼ of a fresh red chilli

1 large firm tomato

½ a bunch of fresh flat-leaf parsley,
leaves picked

200g taglierini
(if making fresh, see pages 16 & 18)

sea salt and freshly ground
black pepper

extra virgin olive oil

zest and juice from ½ an
unwaxed lemon

Parmesan cheese, for grating

Start by preparing your ingredients. Very finely slice the onion, pepper and half the Parma ham. Finely slice the chilli. Quarter the tomato, cut out the seeds and finely dice the flesh. Finely chop the parsley leaves.

Put the finely sliced Parma ham into a large dry frying pan over a high heat and cook for 5 minutes, or until crispy. Transfer to a double layer of kitchen paper to drain. Cook the taglierini in a large pan of boiling salted water until al dente. Meanwhile, return the frying pan to a medium-high heat with 3 tablespoons of oil. Add the onion, pepper and chilli and cook for a minute or so. Roughly slice the remaining Parma ham and add to the pan, stir in most of the parsley leaves and season lightly with salt and pepper.

Reserving some of the cooking water, drain the taglierini and add to the sauce. Add the lemon juice, diced tomato and a good grating of Parmesan. Toss well over the heat until lovely and glossy, adding a splash of the cooking water to loosen, if needed. Divide between your plates, sprinkle over the crispy Parma ham and add an extra grating of Parmesan. Finish by sprinkling over the lemon zest and the rest of the chopped parsley.

SUMMER VEGETABLE CAPPELLACCI

SERVES 4

TOTAL TIME: 1 HOUR
45 MINUTES
PLUS RESTING

sea salt and freshly ground
black pepper

1 x **pasta dough**
(see page 16)

½ x **simple tomato sauce**
(see page 22)

FOR THE FILLING

1 small red pepper

1 small yellow pepper

1 small courgette, trimmed

1 small aubergine, trimmed

½ x 125g ball of mozzarella cheese

½ a bunch of fresh basil,
leaves picked

30g fresh white breadcrumbs

20g Parmesan cheese,
plus extra to serve

For the filling, place the whole peppers on a large griddle pan over a high heat for about 15 minutes, or until blackened all over. Remove to a bowl, cover with clingfilm and cool. Meanwhile, slice the courgette and aubergine lengthways and place on the griddle in a single layer for 2 to 3 minutes, or until charred, turning halfway.

Scrape the blackened skin away from the cooled peppers, then deseed. Finely chop all the vegetables on a large board, tear over the mozzarella and most of the basil leaves, then continue chopping and mixing together. Place in a bowl, add the breadcrumbs and finely grate in the Parmesan. Season with a pinch of salt and pepper, then scrunch well with your hands to combine.

To turn the **pasta dough** and summer vegetable filling into cappellacci, follow the instructions on page 20. Simmer the **simple tomato sauce** over a medium heat. Meanwhile, cook the cappellacci in a large pan of boiling salted water until they rise to the surface, then transfer to the sauce using a slotted spoon. Toss well over the heat until lovely and glossy, adding a splash of the cooking water to loosen, if needed. Serve with a grating of Parmesan and the reserved basil leaves.

This is the perfect recipe for using up leftover grilled vegetables. You can also use this filling to make baked vegetable cannelloni – simply add 2 free-range eggs and an extra handful of breadcrumbs to the mixture. See my baked cannelloni recipe on page 106.

SEAFOOD SPAGHETTI BAKED 'AL CARTOCCIO'

TOTAL TIME: 1 HOUR

3 cloves of garlic, peeled

extra virgin olive oil

8 anchovy fillets

8 king prawns, shells and
heads reserved

1 splash of quality white wine

1 x 400g tin of chopped tomatoes

5 baby octopuses, cleaned

10 baby squid, cleaned

¼ of a fresh red chilli

½ a bunch of fresh flat-leaf parsley,
leaves picked

200g ripe cherry tomatoes

1 tablespoon baby capers, rinsed

400g spaghetti

sea salt and freshly ground
black pepper

100g clams, cleaned

140g mussels, cleaned

1 lemon, to serve

To make the fish stock, chop 1 clove of garlic, then put it into a medium saucepan over a medium-high heat with 2 tablespoons of oil and 2 anchovies. Sweat for 1 minute, then add the prawn heads and shells, mushing them with the back of a spoon to release the juices. Cook for 2 to 3 minutes, add the wine and let it bubble away, then pour in the chopped tomatoes and 1 tin of hot water. Stir well and bring to the boil, then simmer over a low heat for 15 minutes to let the flavours infuse.

Meanwhile, preheat the oven to 220°C/425°F/gas 7. Prepare the cartocci or 'parcels' by cutting out 4 x 30cm squares of greaseproof paper and of tin foil. Lay each piece of paper on top of a piece of foil, then tightly fold up the edges to create a neat border. Next, make an incision along the back of the prawns, scrape out and discard any black bits, then halve lengthways. Halve the octopuses and roughly slice the squid. Finely slice the remaining garlic and anchovies, the chilli and parsley leaves, then halve the tomatoes. Heat 4 tablespoons of oil in a large frying pan over a medium-high heat, add the garlic, chilli, anchovies and capers and sweat for 1 minute. Add the prawns, octopuses and squid for a further 4 minutes, or until just cooked. Strain the stock through a sieve into the pan, pushing the juices through with the base of a ladle. Add the parsley, then simmer over a low heat until slightly reduced.

Meanwhile, cook the spaghetti in a large pan of boiling salted water until very al dente – it'll continue cooking in the oven so it's important to undercook it. Reserving some of the cooking water, drain and add the spaghetti to the sauce along with the clams and mussels (tap any open ones and if they don't close, discard) and tomatoes. Turn the heat up and toss well until the shellfish have opened, discarding any that remain closed. Season to taste, then divide between the cartocci. Pull the edges together and scrunch them up to seal the parcels. Place in the oven for 10 minutes, then carefully open them up and serve with lemon wedges.

TOMATO & MOZZARELLA LINGUINE

SERVES 2

TOTAL TIME: 15 MINUTES

3 cloves of garlic, peeled

optional: ¼ of a fresh red chilli

400g ripe cherry tomatoes

extra virgin olive oil

sea salt and freshly ground
black pepper

½ a bunch of fresh basil,
leaves picked

200g linguine

1 x 125g ball of buffalo
mozzarella cheese

optional: Parmesan cheese, to serve

Finely slice the garlic and chilli (if using) and quarter the tomatoes. Heat 3 tablespoons of oil in a large frying pan over a medium-high heat, then add the garlic and chilli and sweat for 2 minutes. Stir in the tomatoes, season with salt and tear in most of the basil leaves, reserving a few nice leaves to one side. Add a good splash of boiling water, reduce the heat to medium, then cover and cook for 10 minutes, or until the tomatoes have softened.

Meanwhile, cook the linguine in a large pan of boiling salted water until al dente. Reserving some of the cooking water, drain the linguine and add to the sauce. Toss well over the heat until lovely and glossy, adding a splash of the cooking water to loosen, if needed. Tear in half the mozzarella and mix well, then remove from the heat. Divide between your plates, tear over the remaining mozzarella, sprinkle the reserved basil leaves on top, then serve with a twist of pepper and a grating of Parmesan, if you like.

I often cook this *linguine alla Sorentina* when I'm back in my hometown of Minori. There's no need to put your tomatoes in the fridge – here in Italy, we leave them to ripen at room temperature and they taste a lot better! If you can't use really ripe tomatoes, use tinned cherry tomatoes instead.

INVOLTINI OF BEEF
IN TOMATO RAGÙ WITH FUSILLI

SERVES
6

TOTAL TIME: 2 HOURS

extra virgin olive oil

150ml quality red wine

1 onion, peeled

1 stick of celery, trimmed

1 carrot, trimmed

2 x 400g tins of chopped tomatoes

2 tablespoons tomato purée

½ a bunch of fresh basil

480g fusilli
(if making fresh, see pages 16 & 18)

FOR THE INVOLTINI

750g sirloin steaks, fat removed

sea salt and freshly ground
black pepper

20g Parmesan cheese

3 cloves of garlic, peeled

½ a bunch of fresh flat-leaf parsley,
leaves picked

To make the involtini, slice the steaks to give you 12 equal pieces, then place on a board and bash each one with a rolling pin, until about ½cm thick. Season with salt and pepper, grate over the Parmesan, then slice the garlic and sprinkle on top. Layer over the parsley leaves, then tightly roll up each slice of meat, securing with toothpicks or cocktail sticks, and season all over. Heat 5 tablespoons of oil in a large, wide casserole pan over a medium-high heat. Add the involtini and sear all over. Turn the heat up to high, pour in the wine and let it bubble away until reduced by half. Using a slotted spoon, transfer the involtini to a plate and set aside.

Very finely chop the onion, celery and carrot, then add to the pan and return it to a medium-high heat with another 3 tablespoons of oil. Cook for 5 minutes, or until starting to soften, then add the chopped tomatoes and 1 tin of hot water. Refill the tin again and stir in the tomato purée, then pour it into the pan. Cover and bring to the boil. Finely chop and add the basil (including the tender stalks), then season to taste. Cook for a further few minutes, then return the involtini to the pan and bring back to the boil. Reduce the heat to low, cover with the lid askew and cook for about 45 minutes, or until the meat is tender, stirring occasionally.

When the sauce is nearly ready, cook the fusilli in a large pan of boiling salted water until al dente. Transfer the involtini to a plate, remove the toothpicks or cocktail sticks and keep warm. Reserving some of the cooking water, drain the fusilli and add to the sauce. Mix well over the heat until lovely and glossy, adding a splash of the cooking water to loosen, if needed. Serve the pasta as a starter, followed by the involtini with a nice fresh salad.

Involtini works just as well with less noble cuts of beef, such as brisket, shin or feather, just remember to cook them a little longer.

SIMPLE TUNA BUCATINI

SERVES 2

TOTAL TIME: 10 MINUTES

200g bucatini

sea salt

1 large clove of garlic, peeled

1 fresh red chilli

2 anchovy fillets

4 ripe cherry tomatoes

extra virgin olive oil

1 x 180g tin of quality tuna, in olive oil

1 tablespoon baby capers, rinsed

juice from ½ a lemon

100g wild rocket, washed

Cook the bucatini in a large pan of boiling salted water until al dente. Meanwhile, finely slice the garlic and chilli, then roughly chop the anchovies and tomatoes. Heat 3 tablespoons of oil (use the oil from the tin of tuna for added flavour, if you can) in a frying pan over a medium heat, then add the garlic, chilli, anchovies and capers. Fry for 2 minutes, then add the tomatoes and toss well.

Reserving some of the cooking water, drain the bucatini and add to the sauce. Toss well over the heat until lovely and glossy, adding a splash of the cooking water to loosen, if needed. Flake in the tuna, then add some lemon juice and most of the rocket. Toss well to warm the tuna through and wilt the rocket, then season carefully with salt and more lemon juice. Serve with a drizzle of oil, and a scattering of the reserved rocket.

PEPPER & AUBERGINE PENNE

SERVES
2

TOTAL TIME: 30 MINUTES

1 small aubergine, trimmed

extra virgin olive oil

½ a red pepper, deseeded

½ a yellow pepper, deseeded

½ a fresh red chilli

4 cloves of garlic, peeled

6 black olives, stone in

4 tablespoons baby capers, rinsed

200g penne

sea salt and freshly ground
black pepper

8 ripe cherry tomatoes

½ a bunch of fresh basil,
leaves picked

Parmesan cheese, to serve

Halve the aubergine and chop into 1cm cubes. Heat 2 tablespoons of oil in a large frying pan over a medium heat, add the aubergine and fry for 8 minutes, or until soft, stirring occasionally. Remove to a double layer of kitchen paper to drain.

Slice the peppers lengthways into strips, then in half across the middle. Finely slice the chilli and crush the garlic with the palm of your hand. Crush the olives with the palm of your hand, pull out the stones, then tear the flesh in half. Return the frying pan to a medium-high heat and add 2 tablespoons of oil, the peppers, chilli and garlic. Cook for 3 minutes, then add the olives, capers and a good splash of water and cook for a further 4 minutes. Meanwhile, cook the penne in a large pan of boiling salted water until al dente. Quarter the tomatoes and add to the sauce, then tear in most of the basil leaves, reserving a few nice ones. Cover and cook for a further 2 minutes, or until the tomatoes have softened. Add the aubergine, season carefully to taste, then reduce to a lovely sauce, adding a splash of the pasta cooking water to loosen, if needed.

Reserving some of the cooking water, drain the penne and add to the sauce. Toss well over the heat until lovely and glossy, adding a splash of the cooking water to loosen, if needed. Serve with a grating of Parmesan, scattered with the rest of the basil leaves.

> The capers add fantastic flavour to this dish –
> they smell just like the sea. I love them!

OCTOPUS LINGUINE

SERVES
2

TOTAL TIME: 55 MINUTES

12 ripe cherry tomatoes

2 cloves of garlic, peeled

½ a fresh red chilli

2 anchovy fillets

6 black or green olives, stone in

extra virgin olive oil

5 baby octopuses

1 tablespoon baby capers, rinsed

½ a bunch of fresh flat-leaf parsley, leaves picked

200g linguine

sea salt and freshly ground black pepper

optional: ½ a lemon, to serve

Start by preparing your ingredients. Halve the tomatoes, roughly chop the garlic, then finely slice the chilli and anchovies. Crush the olives with the palm of your hand, pull out the stones, then tear the flesh in half.

Heat 4 tablespoons of oil in a medium saucepan over a medium-high heat, then add the octopuses (it may look like a lot but they'll shrink to half the size), tomatoes, garlic, chilli, anchovies, olives, capers and most of the whole parsley leaves. Cover and simmer over a low heat for 40 minutes, or until reduced and smelling good.

When the sauce is nearly ready, cook the linguine in a large pan of boiling salted water until al dente. Reserving some of the cooking water, drain the linguine and add to the sauce. Toss well over the heat until lovely and glossy, adding a splash of the cooking water to loosen, if needed. Very finely slice the reserved parsley leaves. Season the pasta carefully to taste with salt and pepper, and serve with a drizzle of oil, a scattering of the remaining parsley and a lemon wedge, if you like. Fantastic!

> Octopus is delicious – as it shrinks, it lets out all the lovely flavours of the sea. So good!

BAKED TOMATO & CHEESE CONCHIGLIONI

SERVES
4

TOTAL TIME: 1 HOUR
45 MINUTES

20 conchiglioni (120g)

sea salt and freshly ground
black pepper

1½ x 125g balls of
mozzarella cheese

175g quality ricotta cheese
(available at Italian delis)

40g Parmesan cheese

20 large fresh basil leaves

½ x **simple tomato sauce**
(see page 22)

Preheat the oven to 180°C/350°F/gas 4. Cook the conchiglioni in a large pan of boiling salted water until very al dente – it'll continue cooking in the oven, so it's important not to overcook it. Drain well, making sure you empty any water out of the shells, then cool.

To make the filling, finely chop 1 ball of mozzarella and place in a large bowl with the ricotta. Finely grate in half the Parmesan, use your hands to scrunch it all together, then season to taste. Take level tablespoons of the mixture and roll it into balls – you should have 20 altogether. Place each ball in a basil leaf, then put each inside a conchiglioni shell, like you see in the pictures.

Reserving half a ladleful of the **simple tomato sauce**, spoon the rest into a 20cm x 30cm ovenproof dish. Lay the filled pasta shells on top in a single layer, then drizzle over the remaining sauce. Cover with tin foil and place in the oven for 35 to 40 minutes, or until golden and bubbling, removing the foil and tearing over the rest of the mozzarella for the final 15 minutes. Once ready, finely grate over the last bit of Parmesan and return to the oven for a final 2 minutes to melt before serving.

AUTUMN

I love everything about this golden season and all the abundant produce it brings, from pumpkins to wild mushrooms. In autumn, I'll pack up a pasta frittata and head out into the forest for a long day of mushroom foraging.

WILD MUSHROOM TAGLIATELLE

SERVES 2

TOTAL TIME: 15 MINUTES

2 cloves of garlic, peeled

optional: ¼ of a fresh red chilli

200g mixed wild mushrooms, cleaned

extra virgin olive oil

sea salt and freshly ground black pepper

150ml hot organic vegetable stock

200g tagliatelle
(if making fresh, see pages 16 & 18)

4 ripe cherry tomatoes

1 bunch of fresh flat-leaf parsley, leaves picked

Parmesan cheese, to serve

Start by preparing your ingredients. Finely slice the garlic and chilli (if using), then slice or tear up the mushrooms.

Heat 2 tablespoons of oil in a large frying pan over a medium-high heat, then add the garlic and chilli. Sweat for 1 minute, then add the mushrooms and season with salt and pepper. Cook for about 3 minutes to soften them slightly, then pour in the hot stock – it will help to release the mushrooms' beautiful flavour. Reduce the heat to medium and cook for 5 minutes, or until softened and the liquid has reduced by half.

Meanwhile, cook the tagliatelle in a large pan of boiling salted water until al dente. Quarter the tomatoes and finely slice the parsley leaves. Reserving some of the cooking water, drain the tagliatelle and add to the sauce. Toss well over the heat until lovely and glossy, adding a splash of the cooking water to loosen, if needed. Stir in the tomatoes and half the parsley leaves, then season to taste. Serve with a grating of Parmesan and a sprinkling of the remaining parsley leaves.

This is a delicious autumn recipe, especially as it's the season for wild mushrooms. The more variety you can get, the better, so go foraging if you can. Just remember to check everything you pick.

GAME RAVIOLI

SERVES
8

TOTAL TIME: 3 HOURS
30 MINUTES, PLUS RESTING

sea salt and freshly ground
black pepper

2 x **pasta dough** (see page 16)

2 x **simple butter & sage sauce**
(see page 26)

Parmesan cheese, to serve

FOR THE FILLING

extra virgin olive oil

80g higher-welfare smoked
pancetta lardons

1 x 600g whole small wild rabbit or
saddle of hare, jointed

1 x 600g small pheasant, jointed

2 onions, peeled

2 carrots, trimmed

2 sticks of celery, trimmed

6 sprigs of fresh rosemary or thyme
and 1 fresh bay leaf

6 juniper berries

150ml quality red wine

1 litre hot organic vegetable stock

50g fresh white breadcrumbs

For the filling, heat 6 tablespoons of oil in a large, wide pan over a medium-high heat, then add the pancetta and fry for 3 to 4 minutes, or until turning golden. Season the game all over, add to the pan and cook for 10 to 15 minutes, or until browned, turning often. Meanwhile, finely chop the onions, carrots and celery. Add the herbs, juniper berries and wine to the pan and let it bubble away, then stir in the chopped vegetables. Cook for 10 minutes, or until softened, then pour in the hot stock and bring to the boil. Reduce the heat to low and simmer with the lid askew for about 2 hours, or until the liquid has reduced to a lovely, sticky sauce.

Using tongs, remove the game to a board and leave until cool enough to handle. Shred the meat, removing and discarding the bones and skin, then stir back through the ragù. Pick out and discard the herbs, then transfer to a food processor. Add the breadcrumbs and blitz to a smooth mixture.

To turn the **pasta dough** and game filling into ravioli, follow the instructions on page 20. Cook the ravioli in a large pan of boiling salted water until they rise to the surface (do this in two stages to prevent them from sticking). Meanwhile, make the **simple butter & sage sauce**, then use a slotted spoon to add the ravioli to it. Toss together over a low heat for 2 to 3 minutes, or until the sauce is deliciously creamy, adding a splash of the cooking water to loosen, if needed. Serve with a grating of Parmesan.

You'll end up with double the filling you need for this recipe – I like to freeze half ready to fill more ravioli another day. The ragù filling is also delicious just as it is, so feel free to save half (don't add the breadcrumbs or blitz it) and use it in pies or simply tossed through tagliatelle.

VEAL MEATBALLS
WITH TAGLIATELLE

TOTAL TIME: 1 HOUR
40 MINUTES

1 clove of garlic, peeled

1 fresh red chilli

5 sprigs of fresh flat-leaf parsley,
leaves picked

500g veal mince

1 large free-range egg

sea salt and freshly ground
black pepper

30g Parmesan cheese,
plus extra to serve

50g fresh white breadcrumbs

flour, for dusting

extra virgin olive oil

1 onion, peeled

2 carrots, trimmed

1 stick of celery, trimmed

2 x 400g tins of chopped tomatoes

½ a bunch of fresh basil,
leaves picked

600g tagliatelle
(if making fresh, see pages 16 & 18)

To make the meatballs, finely chop the garlic, chilli and parsley leaves, then place them in a large bowl with the veal mince, egg and a pinch of salt and pepper. Finely grate in the Parmesan and mix well. Add the breadcrumbs and use your hands to scrunch it all together. To check for seasoning, tear off and fry a little piece of the mixture. Have a taste, then adjust as needed. Using heaped teaspoons, divide the mixture and roll into balls, then dust them lightly with flour. Heat 2 tablespoons of oil in a large non-stick frying pan over a medium-high heat, add the meatballs and fry for 3 to 5 minutes, or until golden all over, shaking the pan occasionally. Use a slotted spoon to remove them to a plate – they'll cook through properly in the sauce later.

To make the sauce, finely chop the onion, carrots and celery. Return the meatball pan to a medium heat and add 2 tablespoons of oil and the chopped vegetables. Fry for 10 minutes, or until softened, stirring occasionally, then pour in the tomatoes and 1 tin of hot water. Season with salt, finely chop and add the basil leaves, then let it simmer nicely for about 35 minutes, or until reduced – make sure it doesn't thicken too much, as the meatballs need room to swim when you add them later! Once reduced, add the meatballs, turn the heat down to low and cook for a further 20 minutes, or until they're cooked through, topping up with hot water, if needed.

When the ragù is nearly ready, cook the tagliatelle in a large pan of boiling salted water until al dente. Reserving some of the cooking water, drain the tagliatelle and add to the sauce. Toss well over the heat until lovely and glossy, adding a splash of the cooking water to loosen, if needed. Serve with an extra grating of Parmesan.

MUSHROOM RAGÙ
WITH PACCHERI

TOTAL TIME: 1 HOUR
35 MINUTES

30g dried porcini

2 onions, peeled

½ a fresh red chilli

2 sticks of celery, trimmed

2 carrots, trimmed

1 clove of garlic, peeled

extra virgin olive oil

2 fresh sage leaves

1 sprig of fresh thyme

1 sprig of fresh rosemary

1 splash of quality white wine

2 x 400g tins of chopped tomatoes

sea salt and freshly ground
black pepper

700g mixed wild mushrooms,
cleaned

600ml hot organic vegetable stock

600g paccheri

Parmesan cheese, to serve

Start by preparing your ingredients. Place the porcini in a bowl, just cover with lukewarm water and leave to soak. Finely chop the onions, chilli, celery and carrots, then crush the garlic with the palm of your hand.

Heat 6 tablespoons of oil in a large frying pan over a medium-high heat, then add the chopped vegetables, the garlic, sage leaves and herb sprigs. Cook for 10 minutes, or until softened, stirring occasionally. Reserving the soaking liquid, stir in the porcini, then add the wine and let it bubble away. Sieve in the porcini soaking liquid, pour in the chopped tomatoes and add 1 tin of hot water. Season with salt and pepper, bring to the boil, then simmer over a low heat for 30 minutes, or until thickened and reduced. Meanwhile, slice or tear up the mushrooms.

Pour the hot stock into the pan, stir in the mushrooms and bring to the boil. Reduce the heat to low and simmer for a further 30 minutes, or until thickened to a lovely, rich sauce. When the ragù is nearly ready, cook the paccheri in a large pan of boiling salted water until al dente. Pick out and discard the garlic and herb sprigs from the ragù, then, reserving some of the cooking water, drain the paccheri and add to the pan. Toss well over the heat until lovely and glossy, adding a splash of the cooking water to loosen, if needed. Serve with a grating of Parmesan.

BUTTERNUT SQUASH & PANCETTA PENNE

TOTAL TIME: 40 MINUTES

60g higher-welfare slices
of pancetta

3 banana shallots, peeled

½ a fresh red chilli

650g butternut squash,
peeled and deseeded

extra virgin olive oil

2 sprigs of fresh rosemary,
leaves picked

600ml hot organic vegetable stock

400g penne

sea salt and freshly ground
black pepper

10g Parmesan cheese,
plus extra to serve

Start by preparing your ingredients. Finely slice the pancetta, shallots and chilli, then chop the squash into 1cm cubes. Heat 4 tablespoons of oil in a large frying pan over a medium-high heat, add the pancetta and fry for 1 minute, then stir in the shallots, chilli and rosemary leaves. Cook for a further 2 to 3 minutes, then stir in the squash and pour in the hot stock. Bring to the boil, then simmer for 20 minutes, or until the squash is tender and the liquid has reduced slightly.

Meanwhile, cook the penne in a large pan of boiling salted water until very al dente – it'll continue cooking in the sauce so it's important to undercook it. Reserving some of the cooking water, drain the penne and add to the sauce. Stir gently, adding a splash of the cooking water to loosen, if needed, then cook for a further 2 minutes to let the penne soak up all those beautiful flavours. Finely grate in the Parmesan and stir until deliciously creamy. Serve with a twist of pepper and an extra grating of Parmesan.

PUMPKIN & MUSHROOM LASAGNE

SERVES 8-10

TOTAL TIME: 2 HOURS
40 MINUTES, PLUS RESTING

extra virgin olive oil

sea salt and freshly ground
black pepper

1 x **pasta dough** (see page 16)

FOR THE FILLINGS

1.3kg pumpkin or butternut squash,
peeled and deseeded

5 sprigs of fresh rosemary,
leaves picked

800g mixed wild mushrooms,
cleaned

3 cloves of garlic, peeled

½ a bunch of fresh thyme,
leaves picked

FOR THE CHEESE SAUCE

80g unsalted butter

80g plain flour

1.1 litres milk

150g dolcelatte cheese

40g Parmesan cheese,
plus extra for grating

1 whole nutmeg, for grating

Preheat the oven to 220°C/425°F/gas 7. Cut the pumpkin into ½cm slices and place on a large baking tray in a single layer. Drizzle with oil, sprinkle over a few rosemary leaves and season. Place in the oven for 20 to 25 minutes, or until tender. Meanwhile, finely slice the mushrooms, garlic, thyme and remaining rosemary. Heat 5 tablespoons of oil in a large frying pan over a medium-high heat, add the mushrooms, garlic, herbs and a good pinch of salt, and cook for 5 minutes, or until softened, stirring often.

To make the cheese sauce, melt the butter in a small pan over a medium-low heat. Remove from the heat and quickly whisk in the flour until smooth. Gradually whisk in the milk, then return to a medium heat for 4 minutes, or until thickened to a smooth but still loose sauce, whisking constantly. Remove from the heat, stir in the dolcelatte and finely grate in the Parmesan. Add a generous grating of nutmeg and a good pinch of salt and pepper.

Remove the cooked pumpkin from the oven and reduce the temperature to 200°C/400°F/gas 6. Roll out the **pasta dough** into lasagne sheets (see page 18). Blanch for about 30 seconds in a large pan of boiling salted water (3 or 4 at a time), then remove to a clean tea towel to drain in a single layer. Drizzle some of the cheese sauce into a greased 30cm x 40cm ovenproof baking dish, then place a layer of lasagne sheets on top, tearing them to fit like a puzzle. Add another drizzle of cheese sauce, a layer of pumpkin and mushrooms and a good grating of Parmesan. Repeat with another two layers, finishing with a final grating of Parmesan. Cover tightly with tin foil and bake for 40 to 45 minutes, or until golden and bubbling, removing the foil for the last 10 minutes. Serve with an extra grating of Parmesan.

This is a tasty alternative to classic Bolognese lasagne. You can use up leftover cheese instead of dolcelatte, if you like.

SAUSAGE & BROCCOLI SPAGHETTI

TOTAL TIME: 25 MINUTES

250g purple sprouting broccoli

2 cloves of garlic, peeled

½ a fresh red chilli

extra virgin olive oil

200g higher-welfare quality
Italian sausages

1 splash of quality white wine

200g spaghetti

sea salt and freshly ground
black pepper

juice from ½ a lemon

Parmesan cheese, to serve

Start by preparing your ingredients. Remove and reserve any delicate broccoli leaves. Trim and discard the woody ends, then halve any larger stems lengthways. Finely slice the garlic and chilli.

Heat 6 tablespoons of oil in a large frying pan over a medium-high heat, then add the garlic and chilli. Slit open and discard the sausage skins, breaking the meat into the pan. Fry for 2 to 3 minutes, stirring constantly and breaking up the meat with the back of a spoon, then add the wine and let it bubble away. Stir in the broccoli stems and 250ml of hot water, then cover and cook for 10 minutes, or until the broccoli is very tender.

Meanwhile, cook the spaghetti in a large pan of boiling salted water until very al dente – it'll continue cooking in the sauce, so it's important to undercook it. Season the sauce carefully with salt and add any reserved broccoli leaves. Reserving some of the cooking water, drain the spaghetti and add to the pan. Stir gently, adding a splash of the cooking water to loosen, if needed, then cook for a further few minutes to let the spaghetti soak up all those lovely flavours. Add the lemon juice and a twist of pepper, toss well, then serve with a grating of Parmesan and a drizzle of oil.

SLOW-COOKED DUCK PAPPARDELLE

SERVES 4

TOTAL TIME: 3 HOURS

1 x 1.2kg whole duck, jointed

sea salt

1 onion, peeled

1 stick of celery, trimmed

1 carrot, trimmed

225ml quality white wine

2 fresh bay leaves

3 fresh sage leaves

3 sprigs of fresh rosemary

3 sprigs of fresh thyme

2 x 400g tins of chopped tomatoes

500ml hot organic vegetable stock

400g pappardelle
(if making fresh, see pages 16 & 18)

Parmesan cheese, to serve

Place a large frying pan over a high heat, add the duck pieces, season with salt and seal on all sides. Meanwhile, finely chop the onion, celery and carrot. Pour the wine into the pan and quickly cover, as it will spit quite fiercely. Leave to bubble away for 1 minute, then add the chopped vegetables and all the herbs. Reduce the heat to medium and fry for 10 minutes, or until softened, then pour in the tomatoes and hot stock and bring to the boil. Reduce the heat to low, cover and cook for 2 hours, or until the duck is tender, topping up with more hot stock occasionally, if needed.

Using tongs, remove the duck to a plate and leave until cool enough to handle. Meanwhile, skim away and discard any fat from the surface of the ragù, pick out and discard the herbs, then keep warm over a very low heat. Shred the duck meat, removing and discarding the bones and skin, then stir back through the ragù.

Cook the pappardelle in a large pan of boiling salted water until al dente. Reserving some of the cooking water, drain the pappardelle and add to the ragù. Toss well over the heat until lovely and glossy, adding a splash of the cooking water to loosen, if needed. Serve with a grating of Parmesan.

WALNUT PESTO
WITH STRACCETTI

SERVES
4

TOTAL TIME: 25 MINUTES
PLUS RESTING

1 clove of garlic, peeled

sea salt

6 sprigs of fresh marjoram,
leaves picked

100g shelled walnuts

225ml extra virgin olive oil

50g Parmesan cheese,
plus extra to serve

1 x **eggless pasta dough**
(see page 16)

Pound the garlic in a pestle and mortar with a pinch of salt. Add most of the marjoram leaves, reserving a few pretty ones, then roughly chop the walnuts and add to the mortar. Pound well to a rough paste, add 75ml of oil, then pound again. Gradually pour in the remaining oil, stirring and lightly pounding until you have a really loose pesto. Finely grate in the Parmesan, stir well, then transfer half of it to a large bowl (save the rest in an airtight jar in the fridge for up to 2 weeks).

To turn the **eggless pasta dough** into straccetti, see page 18, then cook in a large pan of boiling salted water until al dente. Reserving some of the cooking water, drain the straccetti and add to the bowl of pesto. Toss well, adding a splash of the cooking water to loosen, if needed. Serve immediately, with an extra grating of Parmesan and sprinkled with the reserved marjoram leaves.

I always make double the amount of pesto I need,
ready for a quick meal later in the week – this pesto
is also perfect with penne, farfalle or spaghetti.

SARDINE & SAFFRON BUCATINI

TOTAL TIME: 40 MINUTES

30g sultanas

2 pinches of saffron

1 large fennel bulb, trimmed

sea salt and freshly ground
black pepper

1 onion, peeled

4 anchovy fillets

250g fresh sardine fillets,
cleaned, scaled and pin-boned

20g blanched almonds

400g bucatini

extra virgin olive oil

30g pine nuts

1 tablespoon baby capers, rinsed

1 splash of quality white wine

1 tablespoon quality
dry breadcrumbs

Start by preparing your ingredients. Place the sultanas in a bowl and cover with lukewarm water. Into another bowl, put the saffron and a splash of boiling water, then set aside. Quarter the fennel (reserving any fronds), and blanch in a pan of boiling salted water for 3 to 4 minutes, then remove with a slotted spoon. Finely slice the onion, anchovies and fennel. Roughly chop the sardines. Toast the almonds in a small frying pan and leave to cool.

Return the pan of boiling salted water to a high heat, then cook the bucatini until al dente. Meanwhile, heat 4 tablespoons of oil in a large frying pan over a medium-high heat. Add the onion and anchovies and sweat for 2 to 3 minutes to soften slightly. Drain and add the soaked sultanas, along with the sardines, pine nuts and capers. Cook for a few more minutes, or until the fish is just cooked, then add the wine and let it bubble for a few seconds. Add the fennel, and saffron with its soaking liquid, and allow the flavours to mix together.

Reserving some of the cooking water, drain the bucatini and add to the sauce. Toss well over the heat until lovely and glossy, adding a splash of the cooking water to loosen, if needed. Season carefully to taste, then finely chop and sprinkle over the toasted almonds. Serve with any reserved fennel fronds and the breadcrumbs scattered on top.

WINTER

As the days get shorter and colder, rich game ragùs and cheesy pasta bakes are the only things that'll warm me up.

BAKED CANNELLONI

SERVES
4-6

TOTAL TIME: 2 HOURS

1 onion, peeled

3 fresh sage leaves

extra virgin olive oil

150g beef mince

150g higher-welfare pork mince

sea salt and freshly ground
black pepper

50g higher-welfare salami

1 x **simple tomato sauce**
(see page 22)

250g quality ricotta cheese
(available at Italian delis)

1 large free-range egg

30g fresh white breadcrumbs

10g Parmesan cheese,
plus extra to serve

14–16 cannelloni tubes
(if making fresh, see pages 16 & 18)

Preheat the oven to 200°C/400°F/gas 6. To make the filling, finely chop the onion and sage leaves. Heat 4 tablespoons of oil in a large frying pan over a medium-high heat, add the onion and sage, and sweat for 10 minutes, or until softened, stirring often. Add all the mince and cook for 10 minutes, or until browned all over, stirring and breaking up the meat with the back of a spoon. Remove from the heat, season with salt and pepper, finely chop and stir in the salami, then leave to cool.

Meanwhile, spoon half the **simple tomato sauce** into a 25cm x 30cm ovenproof baking dish. Once the filling has cooled, add the ricotta, egg and breadcrumbs and finely grate in the Parmesan. Use your hands to scrunch it all together, then season. Transfer the mixture to a large piping bag, then squeeze the filling into each cannelloni tube, laying them flat in the dish as you go. Spoon over more tomato sauce – you want to cover the cannelloni without drowning them, so if you don't need it all, use it another day.

Cover the dish tightly with tin foil and bake in the oven for 40 to 50 minutes, or until golden and cooked through, removing the foil for the final 10 minutes. Once ready, add a good grating of Parmesan, return to the oven for 2 minutes to melt, then serve.

GAME RAGÙ 'IN BIANCO'
WITH TAGLIATELLE

SERVES 6-8

TOTAL TIME: 3 HOURS

1 x 800g whole pheasant, boned

350g saddle of wild rabbit
(ask your butcher for the belly
and kidneys too)

1 x 400g leg or haunch
of venison, boned

extra virgin olive oil

1 fresh red chilli

2 fresh bay leaves

3 sprigs of fresh rosemary

6 sprigs of fresh thyme

2 onions, peeled

2 sticks of celery, trimmed

2 carrots, trimmed

150ml quality white wine

1.5 litres hot organic
vegetable stock

600–800g tagliatelle
(if making fresh, see pages 16 & 18)

sea salt and freshly ground
black pepper

Parmesan cheese, to serve

Finely chop all the meat, then place in a large casserole pan over a high heat with 6 tablespoons of oil. Halve the chilli lengthways, leaving it attached at the stem, then add to the pan with all the herbs. Fry for 8 to 10 minutes, or until the meat has browned all over and the liquid has evaporated, stirring occasionally.

Meanwhile, finely chop the onions, celery and carrots. Add the wine to the pan and let it bubble away, then stir in the chopped vegetables. Cook for 10 minutes, or until softened. Pour in the hot stock, bring to the boil, then reduce the heat to low. Simmer with the lid askew for 1 hour 30 minutes, then remove the lid and cook for another 1 hour, or until thickened and reduced.

When the ragù is nearly ready, cook the tagliatelle in a large pan of boiling salted water until al dente. Pick the herb stalks out of the ragù and discard, then season to taste. Reserving some of the cooking water, drain the tagliatelle and add to the ragù. Toss well over the heat until lovely and glossy, adding a splash of the cooking water to loosen, if needed. Serve with a grating of Parmesan.

You can finely chop the meat like I've done here, as I find it adds a richer flavour, but if you want to save time, ask your butcher to coarsely mince it for you.

CLASSIC PASTA & FAGIOLI

SERVES
6–8

TOTAL TIME: 1 HOUR
30 MINUTES, PLUS SOAKING

300g dried cannellini or
borlotti beans

3 cloves of garlic, peeled

1 stick of celery, trimmed
and any leaves reserved

1 bunch of fresh flat-leaf parsley,
leaves picked and stalks reserved

80g ripe cherry tomatoes

½ a fresh red chilli

extra virgin olive oil

130g higher-welfare
.pancetta lardons

6 fresh sage leaves

500ml hot organic vegetable stock

180g leftover dried pasta shapes

100g Parmesan rind (see tip)

1 shallot, peeled

Parmesan cheese, to serve

Soak the beans in plenty of cold water overnight, then drain and rinse. Crush the garlic with the palm of your hand, finely slice the celery and parsley stalks, and quarter the tomatoes. Halve the chilli lengthways, keeping the stem intact. Put 4 tablespoons of oil into a large saucepan over a medium-high heat with the garlic, celery, parsley stalks and pancetta. Sweat for 2 to 3 minutes, or until turning golden, then add the drained beans, sage leaves and chilli. Give it all a good stir, add the tomatoes and cook for 5 minutes to let the flavours mix together. Pour in the hot stock, reduce the heat to low, then cover and simmer for about 50 minutes, or until the beans are cooked, stirring occasionally.

Meanwhile, use a rolling pin to bash the pasta into small pieces (do this in their packets or wrapped in a tea towel). Finely dice the Parmesan rind and very finely slice the shallot. Once the beans are cooked, stir the pasta into the pan, turn the heat up to high and cook until the pasta is al dente.

Take the pan off the heat, stir in the diced Parmesan rind and leave to stand for 5 minutes. It'll start to thicken up slightly, so add a splash of boiling water or hot stock to loosen, if you like – some Italians like it so thick you can stand a wooden spoon in it, but I like it slightly looser. Serve with a grating of Parmesan, the sliced shallot and the reserved parsley and celery leaves sprinkled over. Delicious with toasted ciabatta or a chunk of bread

I always save my Parmesan rinds for winter soups like this one, as they add so much flavour – but if you don't have enough, make up the difference with Parmesan cheese. Eat this the next day either hot or cold – it gets better the longer you leave it.

SWISS CHARD & FONTINA
WITH PIZZOCCHERI

TOTAL TIME: 1 HOUR
10 MINUTES, PLUS RESTING

sea salt

350g King Edward potatoes,
peeled

250g Swiss chard, washed
and trimmed

1 clove of garlic, peeled

100g unsalted butter

150g fontina cheese

60g Parmesan cheese,
plus extra for grating

FOR THE PIZZOCCHERI

200g Tipo 00 flour,
plus extra for dusting

300g buckwheat flour

To make the pizzoccheri, combine the flours and a pinch of salt on a clean work surface or in a large bowl. Make a well in the middle and gradually pour in 250ml of hot water (it should be hot to the touch, but not boiling), mixing constantly to make a rough dough. Lightly dust a board or work surface with flour, then knead the dough by stretching it out with the palm of your hand, rolling it back, then stretching it out again. Keep stretching and rolling it until you get a smooth, soft dough. Pat into a ball, wrap in clingfilm and leave to rest for at least 30 minutes, or until needed.

Meanwhile, prepare your ingredients. Chop the potatoes into 1cm cubes, then finely slice the Swiss chard, including the stalks. Once the dough has rested, turn it into pizzoccheri by following the instructions for making tagliatelle (see page 18).

Put the potatoes and Swiss chard into a large pan of boiling salted water and cook for about 4 minutes, or until tender. Meanwhile, crush the garlic with the palm of your hand and put into a large frying pan over a medium heat with the butter. Chop the fontina into 1cm cubes and finely grate the Parmesan, then add to the butter and allow to melt. Add the pizzoccheri to the potatoes and cook for a further minute, until al dente. Reserving some of the cooking water, drain the pizzoccheri and vegetables and add to the sauce. Toss well over the heat until lovely and glossy, adding a splash of the cooking water to loosen, if needed. Grate over a little extra Parmesan, stir well, then serve immediately.

This is a hearty dish from the mountains in the north of Italy. It's like cheese fondue in pasta form! Pizzoccheri is a type of pasta like tagliatelle, but is made using a mixture of buckwheat and wheat flour – it's traditionally cut into short ribbons, but I prefer them longer. It's up to you what you prefer.

TORTELLINI 'IN BRODO'
WITH LEFTOVER ROAST MEAT

SERVES
6

TOTAL TIME: 1 HOUR
PLUS RESTING

sea salt and freshly ground
black pepper

1 x **pasta dough** (see page 16)

1 litre hot quality organic stock

extra virgin olive oil

optional: fresh flat-leaf parsley or
celery leaves, to serve

FOR THE FILLING

100g leftover roast meat

40g mortadella

1 sprig of fresh rosemary,
leaves picked

2 sprigs of fresh thyme,
leaves picked

2 sprigs of fresh flat-leaf parsley,
leaves picked

1 large free-range egg yolk

1 tablespoon fresh white
breadcrumbs

25g Parmesan cheese,
plus extra to serve

To make the filling, roughly chop or shred the leftover meat, then blitz in a food processor until finely chopped. Roughly chop the mortadella and herb leaves, then add to the processor with the egg yolk and breadcrumbs. Finely grate in the Parmesan, pulse to combine, then season with salt and pepper.

To turn the **pasta dough** and filling into tortellini, follow the instructions on page 20. Simmer the stock in a large pan over a medium heat. Meanwhile, cook the tortellini in a large pan of boiling salted water until they rise to the surface, then transfer to the stock using a slotted spoon. Cook for a further minute so they soak up the beautiful flavours from the stock, then ladle into your bowls. Serve with a grating of Parmesan, a drizzle of oil and celery or parsley leaves scattered on top, if you like.

Tortellini 'in brodo' is a classic Italian starter, but if you want to turn it into a main course, serve it with my **simple butter & sage sauce** (see page 26) instead of stock. If you make your own stock, the flavour here will be even better. Boil up any bones from your leftover roast, skimming away any scum from the surface, then add chopped onion, carrot, celery and bay leaves. Season and simmer for 40 minutes, then sieve. If you do buy ready-made stock, make sure it complements the meat you use.

PESTO CALABRESE

SERVES 6

TOTAL TIME: 10 MINUTES

1 x 260g jar of sun-dried tomatoes in oil, drained

½ a clove of garlic, peeled

2 fresh Calabrian chillies or 3 regular fresh red chillies

2 tablespoons dried oregano

90ml extra virgin olive oil

90ml quality olive oil

Finely chop the sun-dried tomatoes, garlic and chillies, then place in a pestle and mortar with the oregano – the tomatoes are already salty, so you don't need any extra seasoning. Pound well to a smooth paste, then gradually add the oils, stirring and pounding lightly until you get a very loose pesto. Extra virgin olive oil has a strong flavour, so I use a milder-flavoured olive oil to cut through it – quality vegetable oil is also mild, so use that instead, if you like.

Serve the pesto with your favourite pasta (I like penne, farfalle or spaghetti) and a grating of Parmesan, or spread it on bruschetta for a delicious snack – you will love it!

Chillies shouldn't just be used for the heat they give, but for their sweetness and flavour. Calabria is a region in the south of Italy known for its pungent, sweet chillies, so if you can get any of those, I definitely recommend them here!

RADICCHIO & GORGONZOLA
WITH PAGLIA & FIENO TAGLIATELLE

SERVES
4

TOTAL TIME: 25 MINUTES

1 onion, peeled

90g higher-welfare slices
of pancetta

350g radicchio

extra virgin olive oil

600ml hot organic vegetable stock

400g paglia e fieno tagliatelle

sea salt

30g shelled walnuts

80g Gorgonzola cheese

balsamic vinegar

Start by preparing your ingredients. Finely slice the onion and pancetta. Halve the radicchio, cut out and discard the core, then finely shred it. I like radicchio's bitter taste, but if you want to take the edge off, blanch it for 1 to 2 minutes first.

Heat 4 tablespoons of oil in a large frying pan over a medium-high heat, then add the onion and sweat for 3 to 5 minutes, or until starting to soften. Stir in the pancetta, cook for a further 2 minutes, then stir in the radicchio. Pour in the hot stock and simmer for about 5 minutes, or until the radicchio is tender.

Meanwhile, cook the tagliatelle in a large pan of boiling salted water until very al dente – it'll continue cooking in the sauce so it's important to undercook it. Finely chop the walnuts, then crumble or roughly chop the Gorgonzola. Reserving some of the cooking water, drain the tagliatelle and add to the sauce. Stir gently, adding a splash of the cooking water to loosen, if needed, then cook for a further few minutes to let the tagliatelle soak up all those beautiful flavours. Add the Gorgonzola and toss well until the cheese melts and emulsifies into a delicious, creamy sauce. Serve with the walnuts and a drizzle of balsamic. Bellissimo!

Paglia e fieno translates as 'straw and hay' in English. I love how it looks with the red radicchio (a bit like the Italian flag!), but you can use regular tagliatelle, if you prefer.

MUSSEL & ROMANESCO BROCCOLI
WITH CONCHIGLIE

SERVES
4

TOTAL TIME: 40 MINUTES

1 clove of garlic, peeled

500g romanesco broccoli,
outer leaves removed

4 anchovy fillets

1 bunch of spring onions, trimmed

½ a fresh red chilli

1 firm tomato

extra virgin olive oil

1kg fresh mussels, cleaned
and debearded

1 splash of quality white wine

sea salt and freshly ground
black pepper

40g pine nuts

50g sultanas

1 pinch of saffron

400g conchiglie

juice from ½ a lemon

Start by preparing your ingredients. Crush the garlic with the palm of your hand. Break the romanesco into tiny florets, finely slicing the stalks. Finely slice the anchovies, spring onions and chilli. Halve the tomato, cut out the seeds and dice the flesh. Heat 2 tablespoons of oil in a large saucepan over a high heat. Add the garlic, mussels (tap any open ones and if they don't close, discard) and wine, then cover and cook for a few minutes, or until the shells have opened up. Drain the juices through a fine sieve into a large bowl. Discard any mussels that remain closed, then scoop out and add the flesh to the juices, discarding the shells (you can leave a few nice mussels intact, if you like).

Blanch the romanesco for 3 to 4 minutes in a large pan of boiling salted water. Meanwhile, heat 4 tablespoons of oil in a large frying pan over a medium-high heat, add the anchovies and cook until dissolved. Add the spring onions and chilli, sweat for a further minute, then stir in the pine nuts, sultanas, 100ml of hot water and the saffron. Using a slotted spoon, add the romanesco to the pan, reduce the heat and simmer for 5 minutes, or until very tender.

Meanwhile, return the pan of boiling salted water to a high heat and cook the conchiglie until very al dente – it'll continue cooking in the sauce, so it's important to undercook it. Reserving some of the cooking water, drain the conchiglie and add to the sauce. Stir gently, then cook for a few minutes to let the conchiglie absorb all those lovely flavours. Add the mussels and juices, season carefully, then toss well over the heat until lovely and glossy, adding a splash of the reserved cooking water to loosen, if needed. Stir in the diced tomato and lemon juice, then serve with a drizzle of oil.

This recipe comes from Sicily, where pine nuts, sultanas and saffron are commonly used. If you can't find romanesco broccoli, use cauliflower instead.

BAKED FOUR-CHEESE SPIRALI

SERVES
4

TOTAL TIME: 40 MINUTES

30g unsalted butter,
plus extra for greasing

400g spirali

sea salt and freshly ground
black pepper

1 x 150g higher-welfare piece
of cooked ham

80g fontina cheese

80g Taleggio cheese

80g dolcelatte cheese

60g Parmesan cheese

40g shelled walnuts

20g stale white breadcrumbs

extra virgin olive oil

Preheat the oven to 180°C/350°F/gas 4. Grease a 20cm square ovenproof baking dish with a little butter. Cook the spirali in a large pan of boiling salted water until very al dente – it'll continue cooking in the oven so it's important to undercook it.

Meanwhile, cut the ham into cubes and roughly chop the fontina, Taleggio and dolcelatte. Melt the butter in a large frying pan and stir in the ham. Cook for 1 minute, remove the pan from the heat, then add the chopped cheeses and allow to melt, stirring occasionally. Reserving some of the cooking water, drain the spirali and add to the sauce. Toss well, adding a splash of the cooking water to loosen, if needed. Finely grate in two-thirds of the Parmesan and season with a good twist of pepper, then transfer to the prepared baking dish.

Finely chop the walnuts and put them into a bowl with the breadcrumbs and 1 tablespoon of oil. Finely grate in the remaining Parmesan, mix well, then sprinkle over the pasta. Bake for 20 minutes, or until golden and looking fantastic!

This is a great way to use up any leftover cheeses
you have, so use whatever you've got in stock.

TRUFFLE TAGLIATELLE

SERVES
2

TOTAL TIME: 15 MINUTES

20g black truffle

200g tagliatelle
(if making fresh, see pages 16 & 18)

sea salt

200ml hot organic vegetable stock

quality truffle oil

40g unsalted butter

20g Parmesan cheese,
plus extra to serve

Scrape away any dirt from the truffle, then very finely slice it with a knife or coarsely grate it. Cook the tagliatelle in a large pan of boiling salted water until al dente. Meanwhile, pour the hot stock into a large frying pan over a medium-high heat. Add ½ a tablespoon of truffle oil and the butter and let it melt and sizzle.

Reserving some of the cooking water, drain the tagliatelle and add to the sauce. Toss well over the heat until lovely and glossy, adding a splash of the cooking water to loosen, if needed. Add half the shaved truffle and finely grate in the Parmesan, then stir well over the heat until deliciously creamy. Serve with the remaining truffle, an extra grating of Parmesan and a drizzle of truffle oil.

I really wanted to include a truffle pasta as it's such a special treat, especially at Christmas. I love making this for friends who've never tried truffle before, just to see their amazed reactions. It's so good! You can buy truffle from specialist food shops or online.

GRAZIE MILLE!

This book has been such a pleasure to put together and I love it. It wouldn't have been possible without all these incredible people!

Of course, I must first give thanks to my lovely wife, Liz, and my sister, Adriana, for helping me research and write my recipes. To Jodene Jordan, who styled the whole book and made every dish look so beautiful – I used to teach Jodene about 10 years ago when she was an apprentice at Jamie's Fifteen, and look how far she has come. I'm so proud of you!

Of course, to David Loftus – the best photographer there is, and a wonderful friend. Malou Herkes, Rebecca Walker and Bethan O'Connor, the editors – thank you for your patience and for being so efficient! To James Verity, Ash Jordan and Rachael Ball Risk at Superfantastic for designing this book and making it look so incredible. Thanks to Penguin, Annie Lee and Caroline Pretty for copy-editing and proofreading every recipe, and making sure everything is just right.

To Jamie Oliver's Food Team for helping out on the shoots, including the wonderful Ginny Rolfe, as well as Rachel Young, Elspeth Meston, Abi Fawcett and everybody else behind the scenes – you are the best! Ange Morris, what would I have done without you on those early shoot mornings – thank you for looking after me.

A big thank you to all the lovely people at Food Tube, including Louis Norton and Ash Day, for their brilliant hard work and dedication to this amazing foodie network. Why am I cooking soooo good!?

I must also thank Carlo Caporicci, from Tenuta San Pietro a Pettine, for always sending me the best truffles, including the ones featured in this book.

And last but not least, my dear friend, Jamie Oliver, for making all of this happen. You're the most wonderful person in the world.

Grazie mille a tutti!

PENGUIN BOOKS

UK | USA | Canada | Ireland | Australia
India | New Zealand | South Africa

Penguin Books is part of the Penguin Random House
group of companies whose addresses can be found at
global.penguinrandomhouse.com

Penguin
Random House
UK

First published 2015

001

Copyright © Gennaro Contaldo, 2015
Photography © Jamie Oliver Enterprises Limited, 2015

The moral right of the author has been asserted

Jamie Oliver is a registered trade mark

© Jamie Oliver Enterprises, 2013

Jamie Oliver's Food Tube is produced by
Fresh One Productions Limited

Photography by David Loftus

Design by Superfantastic

Colour reproduction by Altaimage Ltd
Printed in China

A CIP catalogue record for this book is available
from the British Library

ISBN: 978-1-405-92109-1

www.penguin.co.uk
www.jamieoliver.com
www.youtube.com/jamieoliver
www.freshone.tv